Uchimata

I P P O N

JUDO MASTERCLASS TECHNIQUES

UCHIMATA

Hitoshi Sugai

IPPON BOOKS

A FIGHTING FILMS COMPANY

First published in 1991 by Ippon Books Ltd
Ippon Books Ltd is a Fighting Films company

Fighting Films Ltd
1 Triangle House
2 Broomhill Road
London SW18 4HX
United Kingdom
Tel: +44 (0)20 8877 1441
Fax: +44 (0)20 8874 8590
www.fightingfilms.com
E-mail: info@fightingfilms.com

Reprinted 2000

British Library Cataloguing in Publication Data

Sugai, Hitoshi
        Uchimata: Judo Masterclass Techniques
        1. Judo
        2. Title
        796.8152
ISBN 0-9518455-1-9

Special thanks go to the GREAT BRITAIN SASAKAWA FOUNDATION for its kind financial assistance
towards the photographs taken at the Kodokan, Tokyo.

Acknowledgements
My thanks go to the Kodokan, Tokyo, for the loan of the dojo for the photographic session, and
Nobutomo Araki, student at Tokai University, who was my capable uke. The photographs were
taken by Britain's leading judo specialist, David Finch, and are notable for their clarity – and the
majority of the contest photos come from his extensive judo library. Additional research for the
history chapter came from many quarters, including Katsuhiko Kashiwazaki of the International
Budo University, Japan, Syd Hoare of the England London Judo Society and Tetsuo Onda, a
former student at Tokai University. I will, of course, always remain indebted to Nobuyuki Sato,
my teacher at Tokai, who was an inspiration for me throughout my student years and my
international career. A special thank you to Duncan Steen for his editing, and to Edward Ferrie
for additional contest photographs and for his unique combination of judo and design
understanding that have combined to produce such effective layouts.

Front cover photograph by Edward Ferrie. Back cover photograph by David Finch.
Typesetting and Design by Edward Ferrie.
Printed and bound in Great Britain

Contents

Foreword

Uchimata is one of the most common throws in the judo repertoire, yet there was no doubt over the choice of author for Judo Masterclass Techniques. Hitoshi Sugai, the Japanese light-heavyweight from Tokai University made an unforgettable impression with his uchimata upon international judo in the world championships of 1985 and 1987 which he won. What is all the more extraordinary is that Sugai does not display obvious characteristics of an outstanding champion. Off the mat, he is diffident in his manner and he is much the same on the mat. Time and time again he surprised his opponents – especially those from abroad, many of whom exhibited greater signs of physical strength and fighting urgency than this slightly chubby man from Tokai. But throughout his career, Sugai was a technician who relied on the basic principles of judo, especially *Ju yoku go o sei suru* (softness overcomes hardness) to win at the highest level. At a time when strength seemed to play an increasingly important part in judo competition, Sugai demonstrated that, in the end, technical excellence and technical precision, when allied to an unswerving fighting spirit, can pay off. It is an ideal we can all strive for.

Nicolas Soames

Masterclass Series Editor.

Uchimata: A Personal View

When I fought for my black belt at the age of fifteen I threw all my opponents with *uchimata*. Over a decade later, I went to Essen, West Germany to defend the world light-heavyweight title I had won two years earlier. I used *uchimata* in four out of the five fights, including the quarter-final, the semi-final and the final against Theo Meijer of Holland. I varied the technique from time to time as I adjusted to the height, stance or physique of my opponents; and of course, my understanding of the throw developed over that period – it is indeed a lifetime's study. But that basic action always remained the same, from start to finish: the feeling of ducking under, or slipping past a defence while spinning in at speed and hoisting my opponent up into the air.

It served me royally through those two world championships and numerous other competitions, both in Japan and elsewhere. During that time I never lost my interest in the throw, and I studied it constantly – checking that my technique was still precise, and keeping an eye open for a new variation, or a new possibility. This vigilance produced its most signal reward after my first world title, when I developed my own variation that was to be seen in quite a spectacular manner in Essen. It began early – almost at the start of my judo career. I liked sport as a child but I was chubby, and while I enjoyed baseball and similar sports, I didn't like running – few fat children do. So I started judo when I was thirteen, at junior high school in Furubita, a small town on the northern Japanese island of Hokkaido where I grew up. At first I did many techniques, including *ashiwaza*, *sode-tsuri-komi-goshi* and even *uchimata sukashi*. But my height indicated a likely physical propensity for *uchimata*, and by the age of fifteen, and my black belt grading, *uchimata* was already beginning to settle. By sixteen, it was my *tokui-waza*, my favourite technique, and although there were times when I harboured a secret desire to be a *seoi-nage* specialist, I had to concede that my body was telling me something completely different.

My teacher at high school was Nobohiro Sato, the elder brother of Nobuyuki Sato who was to become my teacher at Tokai University later. He stressed the diverse forms of *kuzushi*, the breaking of balance, and the crucial role it plays in *uchimata* – as in most other techniques. Time and time again he made me fight against big men in randori, emphasising the high smooth pull on the sleeve grip – *hikite*, as we call it in Japan. He used to tell me repeatedly to pull up no matter how tall my opponent. It was a drill he never allowed me to forget because he insisted on technical precision – which came to be the essence of my judo. He also made me fight against smaller opponents, and always told me to work with the lapel, at the same time instilling a regard for the importance of combinations. It was a wide-ranging but thorough grounding that was to bear immediate fruit in competitions as a teenager, and then as a university student. If you live in Hokkaido as I did you will not find many opportunities for practising with Westerners. I was seventeen when I faced my first foreigner – he was part of a strong visiting Russian team – but I managed to throw him for *ippon* with *uchimata*. Of course at the start I was a bit worried. I was not really a fighter, and I didn't have the kind of power that I knew many Russians developed as a result of their background in sambo wrestling. But I discovered that – curiously perhaps – my judo worked well against powerful opponents. Once I had broken their controlling grip I could slip past their defence and throw them quite easily – or most of them. This was what happened against the Russian in Sapporo – and was to happen many times as my judo life matured.

When I was still seventeen I won the All-Japan High School individual competition at u86k (showa 55), throwing three times with *uchimata* for *ippon*. My training became much more intense when I left Hokkaido at the age of eighteen to enter Tokai University. Tokai had produced a string of champions already and I knew the work would be hard and relentless. I was there while Yasuhiro Yamashita was at his peak, preparing for his world championships in Moscow in 1983 and the Olympic Games in Los Angeles. I admired his *uchimata* although it was very different to mine. With my right grip I was the ideal victim for his famous *ouchi-gari* into *uchimata* combination. He asked me for practices on most days, and only too often I found myself on the receiving end of his technique. Just watching him on television or on video doesn't really show how strong he was when preparing for a big event, or how determined he was once he had decided to throw you. In all the time I practised with him, I threw him cleanly only once – and that was with an *uchimata-sukashi*.

Yamashita was not the only strong member of Tokai's judo club. It was then, and remains now, one of the top dojos in the country and the standard was very high in all weight categories. In addition to normal training, students were obliged to take part in the *kangeiko* (the winter training week, with severe early morning practices) and the *shochugeiko* (the summer training when the heat and the humidity was intense). It was a harsh challenge for me to maintain technical precision in these extreme conditions – for when my level of skill dropped I had little brute strength and aggression to cover up for me. It was also at Tokai that I encountered foreigners on a regular basis, an experience that became invaluable for my international competition career. All the major national teams visited at one time or another – from the Soviet Union, France, East and West Germany, and outstanding individuals from other European countries.

Tokai was home to Austria's Pete Seisenbacher during his training period for both his Olympic titles, and as we were of much the same weight we battled our wa across the *tatami* on many occasions. *Uchimat* was one of his favourite techniques too, though we were very different in our styles. I preferred a rhythmic movement, developed with the help of combinations if necessary, while he favoured a more direct -and certainly more powerful – action. I have similar memories of the remarkable Belgian Robert van de Walle. I must admit that he used to have the upper hand during many of our encounters in the dojo, though when we met in competition it was quite a different story. My memories of university life were not just concerned with *uchimata* and my strong training partners however. I will never forget the winding path up to the Tokai dojo, the rattle of the windows as a hundred black belts trained on its sprung floor, and the sound of the *o-taiko*, the big drum, hammering out the change of practice. It was an environment that was deeply scored into my personality during some of my most formative years, and it will live with me for the rest of my life – perhaps even more vividly than many of the championships I won. Championships, however, provided the essential testing ground for my work at Tokai.

At twenty-one and twenty-two I took part in the Shoriki Cup, the annual international competition in Tokyo. It became clear during the first year that my *chimata* was more effective against Westerners than against top-level Japanese. Part of the reason for this was that my close rivals in Japan knew my *uchimata* and were prepared for it; but it was also that my style of *uchimata* worked best against a strong, aggressive and pushing opponent. And while I specialised in *uchimata*, I also had the rest of my repertoire to draw on – *de-ashi-barai*, *osoto-gari*, *tai-otoshi* and *ouchi-gari*. The following year saw much the same pattern. In the final I faced Bjaarni Fridricksson, the Icelander who was to win a bronze medal in the Los Angeles Olympics. Fridricksson was tall with long legs and long arms, and he took a powerful over-grip. I crouched underneath this dominating stance, spun on the spot, made a strong pull and threw him with *uchimata* in just ten seconds. This was proof, if any were needed, that my kind of judo, relying on technical control, did work against an opponent with a far more imposing physique – which Fridricksson certainly had.

After these Shoriki Cup successes I began to be regarded as a possible representative for Japan in future internationals: all I had to do was to win the main selections. Masako Mihara, who had gone to the Los Angeles Olympics, was still the leading u95k fighter when I met him in the selections for the 1985 world championships held at the fountainhead of judo, the Kodokan. Despite my conviction that my *uchimata* worked best against foreigners, it didn't let me down here. I opened with a variety of techniques – *osoto-gari* (which often worked in Japan where *uchimata* failed), *ouchi-gari*, and *de-ashi-barai* – but then suddenly switched to *uchimata*: Mihara went sailing over the top, just managing to twist out at the end, and conceded *waza–ari*. Again I tried attacking with other techniques, before again producing *uchimata* unexpectedly. Once more Mihara suffered a *waza-ari*, and I had won my place for the 1985 world championships in South Korea.

Above: Hitoshi Sugai on the rostrum at Essen, after successfully defending his world title.

Most Japanese representatives at world championships are under great pressure because everyone – at home and abroad – expects so much of them. As it happened, I didn't feel any particular pressure in Seoul, for Japan had never won the u95k category, and as it was my first time at such a major event, no one really expected me to do it. In fact, things went much more smoothly than I expected. My first four contests were each won with *uchimata* – I was beginning to look as if I were a one-technique fighter – and they each followed a similar pattern: I would have to struggle to get my grip (this was before the new rules of larger judogi), so as soon as I got two hands on my opponent I had to attack. Invariably they went over for *uchimata*.

The fourth round was more testing, for I found myself facing none other than Robert van de Walle, the 1980 Olympic champion who had consistently won medals at major events, and who regularly dominated me in the Tokai Dojo. I was thinking to myself that if he was going to play his normal game of piling on the pressure and pulling me in with unorthodox grips I was going to lose. Instead, after three minutes of this, he had pushed me to the edge when I pulled and threw with *uchimata* for *ippon*. It was almost as satisfying a moment for me as the conclusion to the memorable final against Hyung-Zoo Ha, the Korean Olympic champion. This was an all-action event, with small scores going both ways, until I edged ahead with an *uchimata*. I broke a small bone in my ankle in the process, but managed to limp on, throwing Ha with *tai-otoshi* for *ippon* seconds before the bell.

Though I had done well with *uchimata* in Seoul I knew that there was a real weakness in my technique. All my opponents had been right-handers against my left-hand stance, and these I was able to throw, usually relatively easily. But I knew that I found it much more difficult to make my *uchimata* work in the *ai-yotsu* (similar grips) situation – in my case, left against left.

I wanted to go to the next world championships in Essen in 1987, and then the Olympics in 1988, and I knew that I would inevitably encounter left-handers at some point in this programme, so I had to make good this deficiency in my armoury. One night, after training, I went home and puzzled my way through the problem, which was partly a question of stance, and partly of the opponent's defensive grip on my right sleeve. It was then that I developed the idea of using my opponent's strong grip to my own advantage. It took a little while to get working smoothly, but it was a good idea, and was to be dramatically effective in Essen.

Above: the final of the light-heavyweight class at the 1987 world championships in Essen West Germany. My opponent Theo Meijer of Holland was difficult to grip, so I was forced to attack with only the tsurite grip. Even one-handed uchimata can be surprisingly effective

Once again I didn't feel under any great pressure. I hadn't been regarded as a favourite in Seoul and no-one really thought that I would win the world title for the second consecutive time. Certainly the early rounds were not as easy as in Seoul. My opponents had done their video homework and they were all watching out for *uchimata*.

Their primary defence was to refuse to grip, which was both negative and highly frustrating for me. I had to make a series of one-handed attacks using *ouchi-gari* and *osoto-gari* – and wait for a chance to get a proper grip. My Finnish opponent in the first round, Pasi Lind, did oblige me by gripping and I threw him with left *uchimata*. Aurelio Miguel, the awkward and tough Brazilian never felt dangerous, but had a very good defence and just played the grips. He was penalised for passivity. Dennis Stewart from Britain spent the first three minutes trying to stop me from getting two hands on him, and was penalised all the way up to *keikoku*. Finally realising that he would be given *hansoku make*, he got down to serious udo and I threw him with *uchimata*.

But the going was getting rougher. Marc Meiling from West Germany was a tall and combative opponent, a left-hander like myself, who had the advantage of being on home ground. For two minutes we slugged it out, his power judo against my more rhythmic style. He had his right arm thrown high over my neck, and controlled my left arm. My job was to get control of his left arm so that I could exercise my favoured *hikite* pull, and somehow free my left arm. This was exactly the situation I had thrashed out that night at Tokai, and I was now able to see if my idea would work when it mattered. I swung into the technique and Meiling went up into the air with one of the best *uchimata* I have ever done. This was my most satisfying victory: I had noticed my weakness, found a solution, worked on it and put it into practice at the most important time.

I was now in the final against Meijer, a young but supremely confident Dutch fighter who had done well to get to his first senior world championships final at twenty-one years of age. He too was watching out for my *uchimata*, so I threw him first of all with *de-ashi-barai*, for *yuko* and then switched to *uchimata* – only for another *yuko*, but it was enough to win the title.

Essen proved to be the high point of my career. I was unable to gain medals in either the 1988 Olympics in Seoul or the 1989 world championships in Belgrade. A new generation of fighters had appeared on the scene, notably the Frenchman Stephane Traineau and the Russian Koba Kurtanidze, both power stylists of an extreme kind. However, what could not be gainsaid was that my rhythmic style of *uchimata* had been shown to work at the highest level. I knew that I would never myself acquire that power style – also exemplified by Peter Seisenbacher – though it had certainly proved necessary to at least gain some understanding of it. But I knew too that the Japanese principle of *Ju yoku go o sei suru*, (softness can overcome hardness) can be made a reality, even in these intensely competitive days.

Above: an impressively acrobatic one-handed handstand defence by Britain's Dennis Stewart but it failed to stop this attack scoring ippon!

A History of Uchimata.

Even though *uchimata* is now one of the most effective contest techniques, it appears to have come to prominence relatively late in the development of judo from the ju-jitsu precursors of judo. It exists in *sumo*, where it is called *kakewaza*, but no form of it was included in the first *Gokyo*, the list of forty-two techniques compiled by Jigoro Kano in 1895. However, it was admitted to the revised *Gokyo* published in 1920, where it found a place in the second set, *Dai-ni-kyo-no-waza*, as the eighth technique, following *harai-goshi*.

It is interesting to note that an early name for it was *uchimata-harai-kake*, or *uchimata harai*. However, it was viewed somewhat differently when Kano compiled *nage-no-kata*. It appears as the ninth technique, in the third section which is devoted to leg throws, whereas *harai-goshi* is in the second section, the hip throws. This location in the kata inevitably had a strong influence on the use and development of *uchimata*, especially as judo expanded throughout the world. It laid the emphasis of the throw heavily on the lifting action of the leg against the inner thigh of the opponent.

While *uchimata* may not have been part of Jigoro Kano's judo until the turn of the century, it certainly did exist in the secret scrolls of other schools, including those of the Te Koku Shobu Kai, a ju-jitsu school in the Houki Ryu tradition, which claimed to teach members of the Tokugawa family, the former ruling family of Japan. In 1911 the Te Koku Shobu Kai published in book form its "secret teachings" (though with the admonition that the book was not for sale). The school identified three forms of *uchimata*. These were *ko-uchimata* (small or minor *uchimata*); *taka-uchimata* (high *uchimata*); and *O-uchimata* (large or major *uchimata*).

Though the text is none too clear, it seems these corresponded to the three placings of the lifting leg as follows.

1. *Ko-uchimata*: in a right-handed technique, tori's leg attacks the lower part of uke's left inner thigh(the *nage-no-kata* style).

2. *O-uchimata*: tori's leg attacks the middle of uke's thigh.

3. *Taka-uchimata*: tori's leg attacks uke high on uke's inner thigh – effectively reaping up the middle.

This contrasts with a more modern analysis which sees the three main attacking areas as

1. The classic *uchimata*, where, in a right-handed technique, tori's attacking leg contacts the middle of uke's left inner thigh.

2. The 'hip' *uchimata*, where tori's hip does the main 'uprooting' work, the leg sweeping up the middle as an added effect.

3. The attack on uke's right inner thigh, a little akin to *hane-goshi*.

But the throw has been through many changes as other factors have been taken into account, such as the effects of different gripping. *Uchimata* did not play such a significant role in the very early days of judo, but it came into its own as contest judo developed. It had been brought to prominence by the 1930s, and was one of the top-scoring techniques in the post-war period. Toshiro Daigo, the All-Japan champion in 1951, counted *uchimata* as one of his main techniques, as did Yoshihiko Yoshimatsu, the All-Japan champion of the following three years, and Shokichi Natsui, who won the first world championships held in Tokyo in 1956.

In these early days of international competion, Yoshimatsu was one of the outstanding exponents of *uchimata*: he threw Anton Geesink for *ippon* with *hidari uchimata* in 45 seconds at the 1956 world championships. Also impressive was the middleweight Takeshi Koga who combined an extremely powerful *ouchi-gari* with an agile *uchimata*. In the world championships in Paris in 1961, Koga, who was little more than 80 kilos, met the large and powerful American George Harris who stood at six feet four inches. Koga attacked with *ouchi-gari*. Harris stepped off it confidently, smiling slighty – totally unprepared for Koga's fast spin entry which produced a shattering *uchimata*. But the tables were turned in the

Geesink attacks Kaminaga with uchimata, Paris World Championship final, 1961.

next round when Koga found himself facing Anton Geesink, who had clearly studied the throw after the Yoshimatsu experience. Geesink threw Koga for *ippon* with *uchimata* in just over three minutes with a technique no less impressive than the one with which Koga had dispatched Harris.

During the 1950s, *uchimata* proved the highest scoring technique at competitions in the Kodokan. This was partly caused by the absence of weight categories and the discovery by taller men that the leg form of *uchimata* could be especially effective against smaller opponents. The inevitable result of the throw's success under open-weight conditions was to ensure the predominance of the leg form of *uchimata*, and to highlight *uchimata* as a tall man's throw, which did not do full justice to its potential range of application. Long legs also promoted the use of *ken-ken uchimata*, though this variation was often disparaged as a second-class technique, and referred to as *shomben uchimata*, or the 'urinating dog style'– not the kind of variation that appealed to purists and lovers of fine judo. Yet then, as now, no-one could deny its effectiveness.

The introduction of weight categories did much to expand the use of *uchimata*. It was now possible for a small man to start working on the throw with realistic expectations. One of the first successful smaller men to claim *uchimata* as a main throw was Takehide Nakatani, who won the lightweight category at the Tokyo Olympics in 1964, though he was best known for footsweeps. Hirofumi Matsuda, who won the lightweight category at the world championships in Rio de Janeiro in 1965, was the first world champion from the lighter weight divisions to make *uchimata* his favourite technique. Fighting at 63 kilos, he was just 162 cms in height, but developed a particular style to deal with taller opponents. He used a *kata-eri*, or cross-grip, (more commonly used for *seoi-nage*) together with a prominent hip action. This is now known as the 'Matsuda-style' *uchimata* in Japan.

Takao Kawaguchi, the 1971 world lightweight champion, also used *uchimata* frequently – but by the seventies this was no longer strange: most top competitors had at least one kind of *uchimata* to call upon.

One Japanese study of judo divided fighters into three categories of physical build: tall and thin types, Hercules types, and fat types. It concluded that the first category scarcely used *uchimata* at all. The second category used a leg form of *uchimata*, while the third, the fat category, used a hip *uchimata*. It is not difficult to disprove this, for there are many champions who use both kinds at different times.

Grips and stance have as much to do with determining which kind of *uchimata* will be appropriate as physique does. It must be said also that however much teachers impress upon their pupils the need for a formal two-step entry, nevertheless *mawari-komi* or spin-entry *uchimata*, in its various forms, remains as popular now as it has always been, providing some of the most spectacular executions of the throw to be seen - and the start of some equally spectacular counters! There is no reason to doubt that the throw will continue to be among the most popular for the forseeable future.

One of the earliest examples of Uchimata from the classic Japanese text, "Judo Jitten Nippon Daimashi."

Techniques

There are various reasons why *uchimata* remains one of the most popular techniques in competition and randori. For a start, it is a magnificently dynamic technique, one of the most devastating of all judo throws. In the best instances, a totally committed attack can take both the thrower and the thrown right off the mat, spinning in mid-air before coming back down to hard reality – and the *tatami*. When such a technique takes place the effect is truly breathtaking for participants and observers alike. It does require an ability to balance on one leg, together with a degree of springy action. But this said, it is a relatively easy throw to do on a variety of opponents. It is not necessary to come across very far in front of the opponent's body (as with *harai-goshi*) which means that there is automatically less chance

of being countered. There are, two main counters to *uchimata*: *te-guruma* and *uchimata sukashi*. Although others, such as *uranage* and *yoko-guruma* can be an unpleasant surprise, generally *uchimata* can be attempted with more abandon in competition than would otherwise be altogether sensible against an opponent known to be an effective counter-attacker.

Uchimata is also a very versatile technique. The idea that it is a technique for the larger judoka is time and time again shown to be a largely artificial limitation, born of the days when there were no weight categories. It does work particularly well against a smaller opponent, but with suitable adaptation can be made to work against taller fighters – and certainly against someone of the same size. Nowadays, everyone must study *uchimata* to some extent, even if only to be familiar with the basic strengths and weaknesses of opponents who use it.

One aspect of its versatility is found in the stepping patterns that precede an attack. *Uchimata* can be used by judoka who prefer to pull their opponents on to them, or by judoka who prefer to push their opponents away to make space for the entry. It is possible to pull opponents round to one side, push them round the other side, or set them up with a host of combination techniques. It is also most useful for those who call on sheer power to batter their way through any defence. This may not be the most subtle of actions but it is not to be disdained or ignored – such attacks win many matches.

But I would like to make one essential point at this stage. There are two main reasons why *uchimata* attacks fail – and they have more to do with the hand actions than with the attack or the lifting action with the leg. *Uchimatas* fail because of

    a) A bad *kuzushi*

    b) obstructive grips (which effectively prevent that *kuzushi*). Sort out these two issues, and your *uchimata* will be well on the way. I cannot emphasise this sufficiently. When I come to deal with the techniques, it is inevitable that the photographs will concentrate on the attacking action, with just one or two on the *kuzushi*. But in fact everything is dependent upon the correct breaking of the balance – especially if you are aiming at technical accomplishment rather than a heavy input of power to compensate for lack of *kuzushi*.

This doesn't come easily. Many people say that Japanese judo has a distinctive quality, and after doing judo around the world, I agree. This quality is based on a smooth rhythmical movement which enables a subtle but effective break of balance to be achieved. The resulting throw looks effortless, but a lot of preparation and hard work has gone into it. At first, we learn judo in a methodical manner – one step, two steps, three steps, to ingrain this sense of rhythm. Later, we gradually learn to establish this rhythm within a much smaller range of movement, as few opponents in competition will take three steps so obligingly for us. I cannot pretend that it always works: sometimes this ideal movement is not possible to achieve in competition or even randori. But overall it has proved itself effective in competitive terms over many years, even with increasing worldwide standards; and it is personally and aesthetically highly satisfying. It may seem easier to go hell for leather on the weights, but strength doesn't last for long. Rhythmical judo has greater longevity.

I have divided the techniques into *ai-yotsu*, or same grip (e.g. right hand stance against right) and *kenka-yotsu* or opposite grip (e.g. right hand against left hand stance.) Different stances and different grips all offer their own special problems. The competent judo exponent will know immediately how to accommodate any or all of these particular situations with the requisite techniques.

It may be interesting to note that in competition approximately sixty per cent of successful *uchimata* attacks emerge from the *ai-yotsu* situation, and around forty per cent from *kenka-yotsu*. For some inexplicable reason it was the other way round for me – I vastly preferred, the *kenka-yotsu* situation.

Alexandra Schreiber (West Germany) throw Roswitha Hartl (Austria) for ippon in the middle weight category of the world championships i Vienna in 1984.

Kuzushi
(breaking balance)

The *hikite* (sleeve grip) is the long pull. You should turn your wrist so that the edge of your hand steers upwards, and pull out a little at right angles: this helps to establish movement without working directly against the strong back muscles of your opponent. It is a very small but important point, though most of the action is completed just by turning the hand, edge of the little finger up.

Now comes the strong pull up, leading with your elbow. Have a glance at my demonstrations in the following pages and you will see that my elbow is leading well, and the general direction is up.

The Basic Hand Actions
Hikite (a&b)

(a)This is the all-important sleeve action seen from two different viewpoints. I am pulling high – notice the upward angle. The edge of my right hand is up, my elbow is leading, and I am facing in the direction I mean to take him.

(b) As a result, there is tension along my opponent's jacket. I know he is on his toes.

Tsurite.

The *tsurite* (collar or lapel grip) has been described as the 'short pull'. It should be lifting slightly and push across against the side of my opponent's face. Both the *hikite* and *tsurite* actions should take place together. This is how to achieve a useful *kuzushi*.

(a) There are many kinds of *tsurite* action. This is one of the basic ones, pushing against uke's jaw with the heel of the hand.

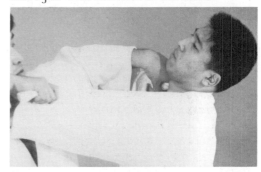

(b) This is another kind, called 'Tenri style' because it was developed at Tenri University. The characteristic feature is the raised elbow, pushing against the jaw. This is quite effective for a tall person against a smaller opponent.

Correct technique means two things: first of all, my whole body is being used in the pulling action (whereas if I pull in to my side, I may be shortening the action, producing a weaker pull); secondly, if I pull down at the start, the danger is that I will do a head dive into the mat.

Uchimata (basic pulling style)
Ai-yotsu (same grips)

> **Keynote** This is perhaps the most common *uchimata*, certainly in Japan. It is the easiest because you can set up the rhythm with a back / forward action. As soon as the opponent reacts to your push by pushing against you, you start your *kuzushi* with your strong pull. It is classical judo.

(a) I have pushed and uke is beginning to push back. I maintain a basic grip – note that I hold his sleeve at the elbow for optimum control. As Uke moves forward, I retreat.

(b) I just stop momentarily, but allowing uke to keep on moving forward. This is just a basic practice, and not part of the real technique: it is there to get the feel of the rhythm being established.

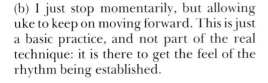

(c) Now, I set off again, retreating on my right foot, my hands pushing down slightly just before beginning the strong pull.

(d) Here's the *kuzushi*. Note my high right elbow, and the pulling action right up from the base of my right leg on the *tatami*. (My left hand is working well too, though it can't be seen in the photo).

(e) I pull uke on to me, with my right elbow still leading, describing a curve. I have not tucked it into my side. My hip is well in, which is what happens with a strong pull in an *ai-yotsu* situation. It can even look a little like *hane-goshi*, though the upward action of the throwing leg will take it up to uke's left inner thigh. See how, although I have hardly begun my lift, uke is already off the tatami - all due to correct *kuzushi* followed by correct body positioning. Very little actual strength is involved in the manoeuvre.

(f) I want a firm base on the standing leg, a good extension from the throwing leg, and a continuation of the turning action. The left hand drives uke into the *tatami*.

Uchimata
(basic pushing style)

Ai-yotsu (same grips)

> **Keynote** The throw is executed against an opponent being pushed backwards in order to create space for the entry.

(a) I push uke firmly – not just with my arms but with my whole body movement.

(d) I twist in, my right leg making a semi-circle behind me so that I can place my foot deep in between uke's feet. I want to feel my hip make contact with his groin. Note the *kuzushi*, and the raised right elbow.

(e) I start to lift with my left leg.

(b) Uke is therefore impelled to retreat.

(c) As his left leg moves backwards, my left foot starts to come across. The timing must be precise while my arms stop his upper body, so that by taking the extra step he is slightly overbalancing forward.

(f) You can see how my leg comes up to uke's inner thigh, toe pointing.

(g) Uke is thrown–note the angle of my supporting leg: my weight is on my flat foot going through the hips.

Mawarikomi - uchimata

Turning

Keynote This is very much the old-style *uchimata*: the principle of a strong turning action led by the *hikite* grip. It is a similar concept to *ken-ken uchimata*, though that is technically based on a *kenka-yotsu* (right grip against left grip) situation.

(a) Uke has started to move, stepping forward on his left foot. I have made a semicircle entry, my right foot tracing a semicircle behind me to put me in this position. If I were to try an entry similar to the one suggested for the pushing *uchimata*, my hip would come out of the main circle.

(b) This is largely about grips. Both my *hikite* and *tsurite* grips are pushing away as I lead uke round in a circle.

(c) I continue the circle to execute the throw, not forgetting to lift with the leg. You can see how this has extended uke beyond the point of no return.

Uchimata (against a taller opponent)

Ai-yotsu

> **Keynote** Most opponents look larger than yourself in competition! In my own case, they actually were, especially in international competition, so I had quite a lot of experience of this technique. The basic idea is to slip past or underneath the defence of the arms.

(a) Using my arms to open up uke's strong defence, I step in deep. The action must be virtually simultaneous. if you make your step even fractionally after relaxing the arms, you will be stopped in your tracks.

(b) As soon as my left foot hits the mat I start to turn and bring my right foot in. Notice how deep I am: once again, my hip is going to play an important role. Also, do not forget to pull well – my right elbow is up in the familiar position and as a result uke is bent well forward.

(c) Against a taller opponent, as in this case, the hip does ninety per cent of the work, with the leg action just adding a finishing touch.

d) The throw.

Uchimata (against a smaller opponent)
Ai-yotsu

> **Keynote** In Japan there are so many open-weight events that we have to know how to adapt our *tokui-waza*, our favourite technique, to all shapes and sizes. The European approach to addressing a smaller opponent is to adopt a power style, with a high grip and dominating stance. The Japanese answer is a little different: the crux of this technique is bounce, bounce, and pulling up all the time.

(c) I bring him on to me. He is nicely settled on my hip here, but the throwing action has a good contribution from the leg – especially with a more resistant opponent.

(a) I push down in order to get an upward reaction.

(b) This reaction helps with the pulling movement as I step backwards, bringing uke with me.

(d) I am pulling well, not trying to hoist him just with the leg alone.

(e) The ideal throwing line – with my toes well pointed, indicating efficient leg action.

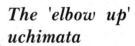

Stephane Traineau (France) got quite a shock at the European Championships in Frankfurt in 1990 when he was thrown for waza-ari by Nikas (Greece) in the opening seconds. He got up, brushed himself down, and then replied with this uchimata for ippon. The moral is: if you are going to upset the tiger, make sure he doesn't get up.

The 'elbow up' uchimata

One variation on the traditional tsurite much employed by western uchimata exponents is that of the raised elbow. This photograph of George Kerr of Scotland exemplifies the skilful application of the raised elbow style of uchimata. This form of grip was initially popularised by Anton Geesink, among others, and it is much utilised in randori when taller players meet smaller partners. It solves the problem of getting under a shorter opponent's defence.

Uchimata (nage-no-kata style)

> **Keynote** This is the traditional method of demonstrating *uchimata*, as it appears in the third section of *nage-no-kata*, the ninth technique of the whole series. It was regarded as a particularly appropriate technique against an opponent who is defending in *jigotai* posture. Once again, the emphasis is on regular rhythm – one, two three.

This version of *uchimata* is still seen at the highest level of competition. One of its most notable exponents in recent years was Ingrid Berghmans, the Belgian world champion, (see opposite).

(a) My object is to pull uke round to my left, using my *tsurite* grip.

(b) My action brings his right leg closer to my lifting leg.

(c) Now, by making a semi-circle with my right leg, I get into position and lift...

Ingrid Berghmans throwing Barbara Classens (West Germany). Berghmans was a waza-ari down with ten seconds to go when she threw with this classic uchimata to win.

(d) and throw.

Uchimata (drawing round)
Ai-yotsu

> **Keynote** This is a freer, randori application of the *nage-no-kata* style *uchimata*.

Berghmans again, this time throwing Tomova (Bulgaria) for ippon in the 1989 European Championships in Helsinki.

(a) There is quite a lot of movement in our exchanges, and I start to inveigle my opponent to my left.

(d) I have brought him so far round that I can actually attack the far leg – uke's left inner thigh.

(e) Normally, in competition, the throw is done on the near leg.

b) As he comes round, I prepare to pivot, aking my right foot back in a semi-circle.

(c) Here comes the attack.

) The throw.

(g) Finish the technique using the arms to drive your opponent into the *tatami*.

Uchimata (Sugai style)
Ai-yotsu

Keynote This was my special answer to the particular problem I faced with *ai-yotsu uchimata*. It was an answer I arrived at between the 1985 world championships and the 1987 event in Essen where it came off so dramatically in the semifinal in Essen against Meiling.

(See Frontspiece)

Fig.1 This was the problem:my opponents would stop my *uchimata* attack dead before I had even started it with this pushing grip on my sleeve. Often, against physically very strong opponents, I couldn't even get my left hand on my opponent's lapel. So, using basic judo principles, instead of fighting it, I go with the flow, pulling my elbow into my side.

(a) This is what happens on the move. I try to take my *tsurite* grip, but uke stops me.

(b) I pull my elbow in and start the circle. A the arm starts to come forward, I begin m turn.

(e)

(f)

Fig.2 Then I pull up with a circular movement. This circle is very important for it enables me to change the direction of uke's push no matter how strong he is – and without him realising what is happening. If you try to do it with a jerk, he will simply let go. Of course if he does let go I can get my grip and do my *uchimata* normally.

Fig.3 Now, I take the arm up high, with the timing very similar to *sode-tsuri-komi-goshi*.

) I use uke's own power to take his hand gh. This time, my *hikite* pull comes in to my est in order to clamp uke to me.

(d) The effect is to twist him – the job that would normally be done by my *tsurite* grip.

)

(e-g) The finish

Note: The opportunity to use this doesn't happen all that often, but it is a useful trick for an *uchimata* expert to have up his sleeve. And it is surprising the number of people who don't let go – even when they are flying through the air.

Uchimata obi – tori
Belt grab style

> **Keynote** This is very much a European technique – it is rarely seen in Japan. Unless done with conviction, it offers a golden opportunity for a *te-guruma* counter.

(c) I pull up with both hands as the hip goes in. There is a strong lifting action from the leg.

(a) I reach over for the belt. I must be prepared for a fast and powerful turn.

(d) It can feel very similar to *hane-goshi*.

(b) Gripping and turning should feel like a single action.

(e) Now, the turning action makes it far more like a *makikomi*.

Two obi-tori uchimata from one contest. Koba Kurtanidze of the Soviet Unon scored waza-ari with his first attack, then modified his technique to score ippon on his American opponent.

nother Russian fighter, Vladimir Dgebouadze, junior world champion at under 71kg, attacks Spinks New Zealand with the belt grip uchimata in the under 78 kg category at the 1991 Barcelona world ampionships.

Uchimata – Makikomi

> **Keynote** This is the traditional response to the opponent who fends off the *tsurite* grip without trying to force it down.

(a) Uke fights the *tsurite* grip, but I have a secure *hikite* grip which is pulling uke on to his left leg.

(a)

(b) My left arm comes over uke's arm. I must get it right over, so that the armpit can clamp on his arm. If I am timid, there is a great danger of an *uranage* counter.

(b)

(c) If I have clamped well, my turning action should take uke up into the air. I don't just collapse on the *tatami*! I am aiming for *ippon* – which means I must turn and lift.

(c)

(d) Uke should feel like a rice-bag on my back which my lifting leg hoists. Even at this point my standing leg is not collapsing.

(d)

(e-f) I keep on turning right to the end.

Fabienne Boffin of France throws Gavrilova of The Soviet Union with uchimata makikomi. Note the extension of the driving leg, a hallmark of a good makikomi.

)

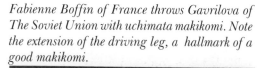

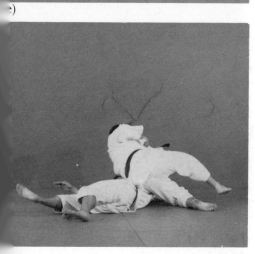

Kata-eri-uchimata

> **Keynote** This is done with a *hikite* grip only. It is really a trick for when I don't want to grip and uke is going wild trying to get his grip because he is behind on a score. I just grab and take.

(a) This posed demonstration shows the action of the hands in detail. The first thing is to grab my opponent's left sleeve with my right hand

(b) As I begin my *hikite* and start to pull and turn, I slap the palm of my left hand into the crook of his elbow.

(c) The pushing action of the left hand is added to the right *hikite* to draw my opponent forwards off-balance as the leg action comes into play. To do an effective throw there has to be good *kuzushi* at this point.

Note I used this technique in the final of the world championships in Essen. I had thrown Theo Meijer (Holland) with *de-ashi-barai* for *yuko*, and he rushed at me to try and get a grip and level the score. It was the perfect scenario for *kata-eri uchimata*.

(a) Now the full technique. I take my sleeve grip in the flurry of action.

b) As I turn, my left hand comes across into the inside of uke's elbow. In a contest, I can do this just to show I am still attacking.

(c) But if I really want to throw, I aim for uke's left leg – I must get well across.

d) Now I pull well with my sleeve grip, but push against uke's inner arm. I want him to be more or less in front of me.

(e) The throw can be very high.

Jumping Uchimata
Ai-yotsu

> **Keynote** This is a little dangerous for competitive use because if you miss, or your opponent sees it coming, you can be caught badly by *uchimata sukashi*.

(a) I step across with the right leg, keeping quite bouncy and springy.

(b) I jump and twist in a flamboyant manner: the very explosion of the movement creates the *kuzushi*.

(c) There is not time for subtle use of the hands, so I have taken a high collar grip with my left hand. This gives me a good base for the pendulum-like action of my leg. Having swung it high, it now starts its descent...

(d,e) and, with extra help from the hip, reaps my opponent right off his feet.

(c)

(a)

(d)

(b)

(e)

Sode-tsuri-komi-goshi with uchimata finish
Ai-yotsu

Keynote If the *sode-tsuri* hip action is not sufficient, the addition of the *uchimata* leg action can complete the throw.

(a) Detail of the *sode-tsuri-komi-goshi* hand position.

(b) The lifting leg uproots uke just enough to give an opportunity to turn him.

(c) Nagy of Romania scores *ippon* with *uchimata* from a double sleeve grip in the under 78 kg category at the 1988 European championships in Pamplona, Spain.

Uchimata

Kenka-yotsu opposite grips

Keynote Facing an opponent with an opposite stance presents its own problems, but in a certain sense it makes *uchimata* easier.

The crucial factor is that the leg to be attacked is nearer – not only for *uchimata*, of course, but for other throws as well, such as *ouchi-gari* and *de-ashi-barai*. The *kuzushi* is also easier. The special problem is the *hikite*. It is more difficult to get a really strong upwards *hikite* pull because of the distance between you and your opponent. And with the *tsurite* grip you must pull up and then punch across hard. But the results, when all this is achieved, can be spectacular.

(a) I start with the inside *tsurite* (lapel) grip. Having started my strong *kuzushi* action, I step in with my left leg, just touching uke's right leg as if for an *ouchi-gari* feint.

(d) If it is done well, high on uke's inner thigh, uke will come right off the ground.

Gennady Tenadze (Soviet Union), shows the usefulness of a lifting elbow action as he throws Dahnani (Algeria) in the lightweight category of the 1989 world championships in Belgrade. Note his left elbow and hand, pulling his opponent on to his toes.

(b) It is really a kind of a guide for me. I accentuate the *hikite* (sleeve grip) pull and then bring the *tsurite* grip into play. Now I can bring the back leg in.

(c) My attacking leg starts to lift uke's right leg.

e) Now my grips bring uke back down to arth.

(f) This is how the hands work. The sleeve grip pulls while the lapel grip pulls up and then across uke's jaw.

Uchimata (against a taller opponent)
Kenka-yotsu (opposite grips)

> **Keynote** There is a certain deception involved here. My opponent takes the high collar grip in dominating fashion. I appear to submit to this treatment, but underneath I keep my distance, ready at a moment's notice to open him up as if I were inside a tent.

Dietmar Lorenz (East Germany) didn't manage a major score with this uchimata against the elusive Frenchman Jean-Luc Rouge in the 1978 European Championships final in Helsinki, but it was the best attack and won the match.

(a) I have the inside grip with my left hand I may be slightly bent over, but the heel of my left hand is controlling my uke. The space between us, the fighting distance, is an important concept in judo. It is called *ma-ai*. Experience tells when the opponent has broken through and is in a dangerous position.

(d) With this base, I can make my turn. duck under any remaining defence, bring my right foot in with the toes well turned The pull with both hands must not be interrupted at any stage.

(b) I come in with an *ouchi-gari* feint, but the leg really acts as a kind of guide.

(c) Once my foot stabilises I can effect my strong *hikite* pull.

(e) Against a much bigger man, I need to use more hip action in the actual throw, my hip going deep into his groin.

(f) The finish.

Uchimata (against the defensive arm)

Kenka-yotsu

Keynote It is important to know how to deal with a hard defensive arm boring into your shoulder without descending to a trial of strength.

(a) This is the problem.

(b) This is the answer.

(c) It is not quite as easy as it looks. The tric[k] is to do it with movement, not strength.

(d) I rock forwards and backwards on the arm to loosen the tension. As the arm starts to bend, I can step in – which helps to distract him from his upper defence.

(g) My elbow points upwards and my wrist bends – in the classic 'Tenri style' against uke's jaw. It is quite a large change of action, but necessary for the completion of the throw.

e) As my foot gets in deeper, I can complete ny destruction of uke's defence. It is a kind of double attack. As soon as my left foot ouches the mat my right foot comes in.

(h) The see-saw action of my head dipping and leg swinging up the middle launch uke into the air.

) Now, my right elbow and wrist start to lift.

(i) *Ippon*!

Uchimata
(European power style)
Kenka-yotsu

> **Keynote** Peter Seisenbacher, Olympic middleweight champion in 1984 and 1988, had an exceptionally powerful *uchimata*, stepping in deep – left foot first, then right. He preferred to operate from a high collar grip, using his height and strength – and personality – to pull his opponent's head down

a) Even against a defensive opponent, Seisenbacher powers his way into position.

Note This is not a pretty technique but it is realistic and, without doubt, effective. It is a form of *uchimata* that is seen regularly both at club level and at the main international competitions.

(d) Now Seisenbacher starts to dip his head towards the floor. Note the strong working action of both hands, while the lifting leg stretches his opponent beyond the point of no return.

A dynamic uchimata from Ben Spijkers (Holland) against Vitaly Pesniak (Soviet Union) in the middleweight category of the 1986 European Championships in Belgrade, Yugoslavia. Waza-ari scored.

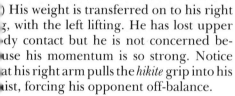

) His weight is transferred on to his right
ʒ, with the left lifting. He has lost upper
·dy contact but he is not concerned be-
use his momentum is so strong. Notice
at his right arm pulls the *hikite* grip into his
·ist, forcing his opponent off-balance.

(c) Seisenbacher starts a strong twist – he
goes through ninety degrees, hopping his
way round, and taking his adversary off-
balance with each hop. Uke is taken over his
own supporting leg.

Seisenbacher adds an extra spring to the
chnique as his opponent goes over the
·tside edge of his foot.

(f) The fall is severe, with Seisenbacher landing on his victim to ensure *ippon*.

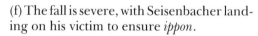

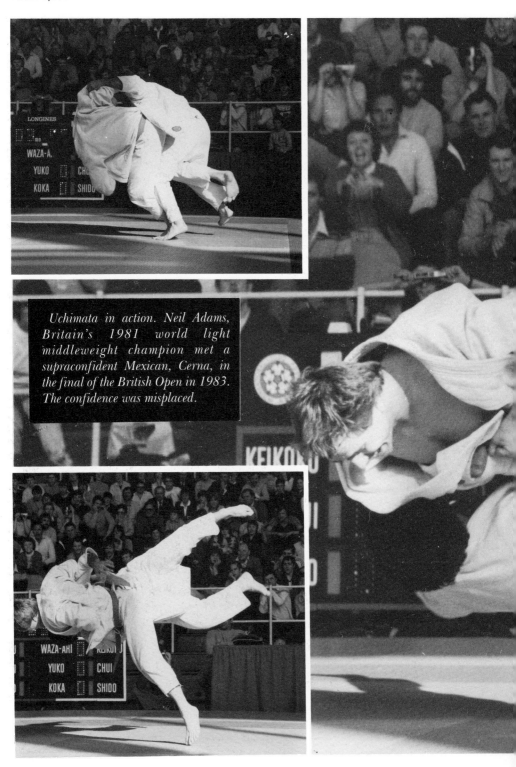

Uchimata in action. Neil Adams, Britain's 1981 world light middleweight champion met a supraconfident Mexican, Cerna, in the final of the British Open in 1983. The confidence was misplaced.

a) With the inside grip, Adams is in the perfect position to unleash his uchimata. b) He starts to lift. Cerna, feeling the danger as he is hoisted into the air, tries to prevent being rolled over by putting his left arm around Adams' waist. c) It doesn't work – Adams pulls him round with the sleeve grip. d) The total commitment by Adams is evident as both players come high off the ground. e) An incontrovertible ippon.

Uchimata (grip round the back)
Kenka-yotsu (opposite grips)

> **Keynote** This too is useful against an opponent who holds with a strong high collar grip. Again, there is an element of deception: I try to fend off that top grip, but eventually make it appear as if he has won it and gained the dominating position.

(a) I try to hold off the attack.

(d) I step in, pulling my opponent on to my hip. Note the toes of my right foot pointing away, in the direction of my throw.

(e) If he is not going to go with the hip alone I bring the leg action in to play, right up the middle.

(b) I resist my opponent's efforts to pull me in to him by keeping my left arm stiff. I have a good grip on his sleeve with my right hand.

(c) I change grip, slipping my left arm under his armpit and turn in under the outstretched arm. I am looking for good hip contact.

(f) My left wrist bends upwards on his back in a kind of 'Tenri style' action. This gives extra power.

(g) The throw.

Kata-eri-uchimata
Kenka-yotsu

Keynote This is slightly different to the *ai-yotsu* version I used against Meijer in Essen (see p.36). This feels much more like *seoi-nage*: it was a speciality of Hirofumi Matsuda, world lightweight champion in Rio de Janeiro in 1965.

Hand action

(a) I take a grip on one side.

(b) I push up with my knuckles making contact under uke's chin, so that it feels a little like a *kouchi-gari* attack.

(c) This makes him push forward in defence, and I can make my attack. Once again, it is a technique that depends upon a smooth but controlled rhythm.

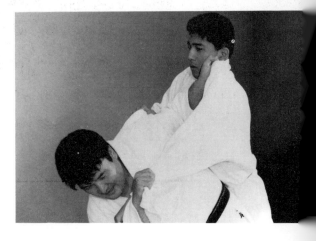

(d) Now you can see that I start to turn immediately after that *kouchi-gari* feint – there must be no hesitation: I come in as soon as I feel him pushing against me.

(e) My actual throwing position feels like *seoi-nage* – the traditional back-carry posture.

f) There is a lot of contact all along the leg - it can even feel a little like *hane-goshi*.

(g) The finish.

Uchimata
(one-arm attack)
Kenka-yotsu

Keynote This has been used with notable success in the past by fighters such as Peter Seisenbacher, (see below) but as it came very close to throwing with an armlock, the IJF has tightened the rules. It is now forbidden to go down to the ground with this kind of technique (ending up in an uncontrolled *waki-gatame* situation), though it is allowable if there is a clear intention to throw.

(a) The *kenka-yotsu* stance. I take hold of my opponent's sleeve with my right hand.

Peter Seisenbacher scores with a one-handed uchimata attack on Bob Berland of the USA in the final of the Olympic Games, Los Angeles 1984.

(d) My left elbow forces the *kuzushi*.

(b) I pivot in.

(c) The *uchimata* attack begins.

(e) To throw, I need a good rotation, turning to my right. Uke is now about to go, and not even his outstretched hand can stop him.

(f) The finish. Generally, this attack only produces a *koka* or *yuko* score – which may just be enough to win a contest.

Uchimata
Russian belt-grab style
Ai-yotsu

> **Keynote** This is a power technique –
> a variation on *makikomi* – used by
> Russian fighters in particular.

(a) I can grip my judogi or even my belt, as
here. The idea is to pin uke's body to mine.
I want to trap his arm above his elbow.
(b) I take grip and stand in position for the
entry.
(c,d) I twist in, and launching myself forward, take uke with me.
(e,f) The landing is not very pleasant for
uke.
(g) *Ippon*!

(a)

(b)

(c)

(d)

(e)

Hansoku-make
Disqualification

> **Keynote** This is the great danger of *uchimata*: a head dive where tori can damage his neck or spine badly. This has caused some deaths in judo and any tendency to do it should be vigilantly controlled.

(a) The *uchimata* attack without *kuzushi*.

(b, c) Tori wildly throws himself forward and lands on the back of his neck.

(a)

(b)

(c)

)

(g)

a) Jason Morris (USA) slips past the strong defence of F. Ayala (Chile) in the light middleweight category of the world championships in Barcelona in 1991, and takes him well off the ground in a classic uchimata manner.

b) Extending on the tips of his toes, Morris turns Ayala and shows superb control and balance in the heat of contest..

c) Ippon! Morris's right hand plants his opponent flat on the back of his shoulders.

a) *Morris discovered what it is like to be thrown for ippon with uchimata in the very next round. Facing Johann Laats (Belgium), he found himself up in the air, astride a strongly lifting leg.*

b) *He tries to wriggle off it, but is foiled by Laat's good control of Morris's upper body with the two sleeve grips. The grip is almost like a rope around Morris's upper body, preventing him twisting out.*

Combinations

Looking at the records of many leading *uchimata* specialists over the years it seems as if all they have ever done is *uchimata*. If I look at my own record in competition in the world championships alone, it appears that I concentrated almost exclusively on *uchimata*, only slipping in the occasional *tai-otoshi* or *de-ashi-barai* from time to time. But this is not true.

I reckon that seventy per cent of my *uchimata* successes came from combinations, even though the final technique may have been *uchimata*. Sometimes the *uchimata* may have been the result of a direct combination, opening with *ouchi-gari* or *de-ashi-barai*. Sometimes, the combination process was more subtle, with my opponent being coaxed to forget about my *uchimata* with a string of other reasonable techniques until his defences had dropped and I could attack. A combination, therefore, can be a true follow-on technique, or it can be a string of tech-

niques stretching over half of the contest. This psychological use of combinations is very important, and worth a study of its own.

Though I cannot prove it with a sheaf of figures, I believe that almost all my *uchimata* techniques against left-handed opponents – i.e. in the *kenka-yotsu* situation – were really the result of a combination. I have said earlier that an opponent holding the opposite grip really offers himself as an *uchimata* target because the leg to be attacked is so close. However, it must be said that he is only too acutely aware of this: the defence antennae are specially attuned to danger signals on that leading leg, and to make a successful direct attack is not easy.

This is where combinations come in. The first fundamental purpose of the *uchimata* combination is to disguise the real attack so that your opponent drops his defences. The second fundamental purpose to make your opponent produce the break of balance virtually by himself, allowing the *uchimata* to proceed smoothly.

Of course, it can happen the other way round too – a strong threat with *uchimata* resulting in an entirely different throw. One of the clearest examples of this is the *uchimata/ kosoto-gari* (or *de-ashi-barai*) 'twitch' where you threaten with a powerful *uchimata*, perhaps really trying to throw once or twice, and then suddenly tori flicks the hip and leg as if coming across for another *uchimata* – only to switch back for *kosoto-gari*. The impact of that combination can produce a devastating throw which is totally effortless. This is what combinations are all about: an ideal way to confuse, open and conquer seemingly impenetrable defences.

Knorrek of East Germany throws Asenov of Bulgaria to win the bronze medal in the under 95 kg class at the European Championships in Prague 1991.

Kouchi-gari into uchimata

Ai-yotsu

Keynote This is one of the most popular standard combinations – *kouchi-gari* works well as an 'opener' for a host of throws. Not only does it pry open a defence, but it allows you to get into a rhythm which your opponent cannot stop.

(a) I push uke backwards to impose my rhythm. Notice that I am coming forward with my whole body – I am not just pecking at the foot.

(d) Uke, still reacting to the *kouchi-gari*, pushes forward slightly – which is just what I want to happen. He is kindly providing me with my *kuzushi* just as my right leg starts to move into position.

(e) My hips come in...

(b) Uke must retreat, and I start to clip at his left foot.

(c) Uke takes his foot away from danger and, more often than not, freezes momentarily. I am already starting my main attack.

) and the throw proceeds as normal.

(g) *Ippon!*

Ouchi-gari into uchimata 1

Ai-yotsu and *kenka-yotsu*

Keynote This is the most popular kind of combination in competiton: a forceful backwards/forwards routine. This is the large-scale version, though it works in a number of modified, shortened styles. A large, slow opponent may need to be encouraged to make all these movements, while a fast, nervous opponent will react just to a suggestion of an *ouchi-gari* leg attack. The principle, however, remains the same.

(a) I push uke backwards to establish rhythm between us.

(d) As uke steps off it, and backwards, follow, precisely matching our timing.

(g) The hip contact is deep.

(b) I step across in formal manner for my *ouchi-gari*.

(c) I flick my left leg against uke's calf.

(e) Note how his right foot and my left foot have hit the ground together.

(f) Now I have a base for my *uchimata* pivot entry.

(h)The momentum is such that an overthrow is a real possibility.

(i) Overthrow!

Ouchi-gari into uchimata 2

Kenka-yotsu

Keynote This is the *ouchi-gari-uchimata* version made famous by Yasuhiro Yamashita, world and Olympic champion, perhaps the most famous graduate from Tokai University . He used it very effectively throughout his competition career, throwing many, much taller opponents with it. The essence of the throw is to retain good balance yourself while breaking your opponent's balance at a particular angle.

(a) Notice the *kenka-yotsu* stance. I have the inside grip. I hook the leg in a manner that could suggest either *ouchi-gari* or *uchimata.*

(b) I feel for my opponent's weak angle. I start a bouncing action going – at this point I could switch either back or forwards.

(c) I start to pull him round towards *uchimata* in a kind of *ken-ken* style.

Yasuhiro Yamashita attacking Robert van de Walle in the 1981 world championships with uchimata. The Belgian just prevented a score by twisting free.

d) Now, I am committed to this curious *uchi/uchimata* combined throw. My opponent can lift his leg high, and probably feels quite safe.

(e) But I am directing him increasingly onto the outside edge of his left foot. This is the crucial point. It may need a bit of a pull or a bit of a push. It feels a little like a driving manoeuvre, like getting a car into the right parking spot. It is actually more difficult than it looks, but when your opponent gets to the point of no return, it is a crushing fall.

Sasae-tsuri-komi-ashi into uchimata.

Ai-yotsu

> **Keynote** This calls for a *kenka-yotsu* stance with the *ai-yotsu* grip, to bring the leg to be attacked closer to you. This means that the actual throwing action is heavily dependent upon a firmly lifting leg.

(a) I step to the front with my right foot to get uke moving in the right direction.

(b) I attack with *sasae-tsuri-komi-ashi*, pulling well with my *tsurite* grip.

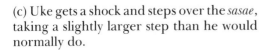

(c) Uke gets a shock and steps over the *sasae*, taking a slightly larger step than he would normally do.

g) It is necessary to understand that this chimata uses the attacking leg much more than the hip in the throwing action. If you try to come across with the hip in this situation, you run a risk of being countered.

(f) I attack and throw.

d) Now I am in the position to launch my chimata attack – and notice how uke is perfectly placed.

(e) My right leg describes a semi-circle to finally place my right foot (the standing leg) slightly outside uke's right foot.

Uchimata into kouchi-gari
Ai-yotsu

> **Keynote** The starting signal for this switch in attack is, a) your opponent lifting his leg in the air to avoid the *uchimata*; or b) an opponent who defends by simply blocking hard, bringing his hips forward.

a) I enter for *uchimata*, and uke lifts his leg.

(b) I keep on trying to make him feel that he is losing his balance, and that as soon as he gets his leg to the ground he must lean back a bit to regain it.

(c) Uke gets off the throw. Now the work of the hands becomes important: my *tsurite* (lapel) grip must change to a kind of upper-cut, as it would normally do for a *kouchi-gari*. It tips him backwards slightly.

(d) Now I can bring the leg down quickly and slice his foot from beneath him. Note the direction of the throw.

(e) The finish.

Uchimata into ouchi-gari
Ai-yotsu

(a)

> **Keynote** This would seem an obvious combination because with the opponent's leg hooked, one can ring the changes between a backwards and a forward technique. But there is a real danger of being countered if the attacks are sloppy.

(a) The *uchimata* is not going to work, and the switch of attack is beginning.

(b) I change direction – not only with my head and body, but with my standing leg as well. Look how my right foot has turned, and how I have established a firm base to push from. My face looks directly at uke.

(c,d) I am committing myself totally to *ouchi-gari* – there is nothing equivocal about it.

Note The signal to decide whether to switch to *kouchi-gari* or to *ouchi-gari* lies in the placing of your opponent's left foot. If it is on a level or in front of your standing leg, switch to *kouchi-gari*. If it is behind your standing leg, you can switch to *ouchi-gari*.

(b)

c)

(d)

Uchimata into tani-otoshi

Kenka-yotsu

> **Keynote** This is a technique which I use when I am too close to do an effective footsweep.

(a) The *uchimata* feint. Notice my hip just flicking forward.

(b) I change direction.

(c) My left leg stretches out as far as possible...

(d) And then clips back in a scything action. Note how I am still pushing strongly off my right leg. Equally important is the right hand action, forcing his arm across his face. This prevents any possible last-second *ouchi-gari* counter.

(e) I take him right down to the ground.

(f) This is a strong position for *ne-waza* if the score is less than *ippon*.

Uchimata into de-ashi-barai
Ai-yotsu or *kenka-yotsu*

> **Keynote** This is the classic feint against someone who is expecting an *uchimata*. In rugby parlance, you are selling your opponent a dummy.

(a) I have brought my hip across a number of times, and now I am ready to switch.

(a)

(b) Uke brings his right hip forward to block yet another *uchimata* attack – only I am ready with my footsweep.

(b)

(c,d) Over he goes.

(c)

(d)

Defences and Counters

Unless combinations are used to disguise it, *uchimata* can be predictable. This should make it quite an easy technique to stop or counter, but the very nature of the move – attacking inside the opponent's defences – means that there is a real danger in waiting to counter *uchimata*.

There are some memorable stories of counters that have worked and counters that have failed. In the semi-final of the 65k category in the 1981 world championships, Katsuhiko Kashiwazaki faced one of his main rivals, East Germany's Torsten Reissman, a known left-handed *uchimata* specialist. After about three minutes, Kashiwazaki scored *oka* with a small footsweep, and they both rolled out of the area in the process. He reported afterwards how he happened to see Reissman's eyes as he got up: "He was obviously furious to be caught like that, and I just felt that he would now attack with his strongest throw – *uchimata*." As soon as they took grip, Reissman came steaming in for left *uchimata* as predicted. Kashiwazaki had

his optimum grip and stance, neatly side-stepped the attacking leg, and countered the German with a perfect *uchimata sukashi* for *ippon*. He went on to win the title.

That was one tale of success in countering *uchimata*. Karen Briggs, Britain's four-times world champion, has a less happy memory. Fighting in the Austrian Open one year, she met the tall Kerstin Emich, another German who specialised in *uchimata*. Emich attacked and Briggs, anticipating her, bent down to pick her up with *te-guruma*. But the world champion, misjudging the length of Emich's legs, was unable to disentangle herself. Emich continued to hop and pull, and over went Briggs for *ippon* – not something that happened to her very often in her outstanding career.

These two incidents illustrate the dangers of counters – for both participants. Of course, a sloppy, indecisive *uchimata* can be punished quite easily. But it is easier, certainly safer, to stop it before it gets going than to rely on a counter.

(a) In the 1981 world championships in Maastricht, Seisenbacher attacks Bodaveli (USSR) with uchimata. Bodaveli stops the throw by pulling hard with his left hand on the lapel.

(b) Seisenbacher begins to feel unstable and lets go of his sleeve grip. Bodaveli prepares for the counter.

(c) He starts his powerful lifting action for uranage. Seisenbacher, showing good awareness, grabs the trouser leg to try and stop the big suplex action.

(d) However he is not yet a match for such superb Russian skill, and flies for ippon.

Defences

> **Keynote** There are three simple defences, and they need to be appreciated by everyone – not least the *uchimata* specialist himself. He needs to know, more than anyone, what he will have to contend with.

Defence 1

Simply push the *tsurite* (lapel) hand down. Take it well into your opponent's own hip – this prevents any effective movement at all.

Defence 2

This involves blocking with the hip. I bring forward my hip to prevent the thrower bending me forward on to the throw. Notice how my right hand has gone around my opponent's waist to make the block all the safer. However, it should be said that there are many photos of players for whom this defence has been insufficient, being thrown high and heavy – with the arm clearly around the waist.

Defence 3

Breaking your opponent's *hikite* grip means that he simply cannot pull you on to the throw. He may be able to jack you up if his attack is very determined, but he will almost certainly be unable to turn you in the air to put you on your back. Not elegant, but effective.

Uchimata sukashi (slip)
Kenka-yotsu

Keynote This is not only elegant and economical, but it actually works at the very highest level, as Olympic and world championship results attest. Once again, any *uchimata* specialist must have a good understanding of this technique. It calls for good balance, fine hand control and a cool nerve.

(a) Uke attacks me with *uchimata*. Before he does so I must know that I am going to use *uchimata sukashi*. Any indecision on my part will be disastrous

Shinji Hosokawa of Japan scores ippon with uchimata sukashi on Bartolemou Dias of Angola, Seoul Olympic games, 1988.

(b) I let him make his attack, subtly keeping it under control with my hands.

(c) As my knee comes up to avoid the throw I lean in on my opponent. That bent knee the crucial point.

) With uke's impetus still taking him into
e throw, I take over control. My sleeve
ip starts to pull strongly.

(g) By bending the knee and getting the foot
out of the way, I prevent uke hooking the
leg.

Now my lapel grip starts to push and uke
ns on to his back.

One of the finest uchimata sukashi in world judo.
Katsuhiko Kashiwazaki, Japan's featherweight in
the 1981 world championships in Maastricht, avoids
and then counters Torsten Reissman for ippon.

I am ready to follow into *ne-waza* if *ippon*
1ot given.

(h)Detail of hand action.

Uchimata sukashi

Ai-yotsu

> **Keynote** Most successful *uchimata sukashi* come from a *kenka-yotsu* situation (opposite grips).

(a) My opponent attacks with *uchimata*.

(c) Now I can come back into position for attack.

(b) I step backwards, avoiding the attacking leg.

(d) I complete the turn.

Note: While it is possible to do an *ai-yotsu sukashi*, it is quite dangerous: I once threw main rival with it in Japan, but I was no happy to use it often. If your avoidanc action is imprecise, you can get caught badl

Uchimata countered by tai-otoshi
Kenka-yotsu

> **Keynote** This is much the same as *uchimata sukashi*, only slower – but safer.

(a) Having avoided, I come across with the leg.

(b) I can now control uke all the way down to the ground, even if his attack hasn't been sufficiently abandoned to make him throw himself.

(c) The throw is brought off very much by turning the upper body and hands, rather than by making use of the springing action of the leg as some *tai-otoshi* experts advocate in a direct attack.

Uchimata countered by te-guruma

Ai-yotsu or kenka-yotsu

> **Keynote** If *sukashi* is the most popular counter for *uchimata* in Japan, *te-guruma* is the most popular counter in the West – partly because of the preparation for this kind of power technique. The opportunity arises when the *uchimata* attack is made without correct *kuzushi*.

(a) Uke attacks, but with poor *kuzushi*. I prepare to counter by sinking my weight and blocking with my hips.

(d) Having reached the top of the swing, my left hand starts to pull down.

(e) The circling motion is helped by the lifting knee – I can pivot my opponent over my hip.

(b) I start the pick-up, not forgetting to pull on the sleeve grip.

(c) I lift correctly, thrusting my hips forward. This not only takes the weight off my back and allows me to lift someone of my own weight easily, but also brings his attacking leg clear so that I can unload him.

f)It is very important that my left hand pulls round strongly on his lapel to ensure that uke lands on his back and not his head.

(g) The right hand pulls uke's legs up high and releases, dropping him flat on his back.

Uchimata countered by uchimata

Kenka-yotsu

> **Keynote** This is another kind of avoidance counter, but it is a bit risky, and needs confidence to execute it well.

Detail of step and foot positions.

(a) Uke attacks.

(d) By pushing his leg down to the ground and establishing my own base I break uke's balance. This is accentuated by pulling hard on the *hikite* grip, bringing uke round.

(e) Now I can attack with my *uchimata*. And from what appeared a very unstable and even unpromising position comes a spectacular throw. It is like a spring uncoiling.

(b) I have anticipated it and started my avoidance. I need to clear both my left leg and my hands in order not to be caught.

(c) My left leg drives down, making firm contact with uke's leg.

(f) Having stepped hard onto my left foot I can now jump through onto my right leg and begin to drive my left leg upwards.

(g) The tables are totally turned.

Ouchi-gari countered by uchimata

Kenka-yotsu

Keynote This comes out of nice, fluid open judo – the kind one finds more in randori than in the tense environment of competition. But it is a movement which teaches and promotes smooth judo action and a bold attitude towards the use of *uchimata*.

(c) I step off the attack, and turn without pausing in a big semi-circular motion.

(a) Uke attacks with *ouchi-gari*.

(d) Uke effectively walks straight on to the *uchimata*.

(b) Instead of resisting the push I go with it.

(e) By adding the power of my pulling action to his push the resulting throw is dynamic

(a) My opponent attacks with drop *seoi-nage*.

Drop seoinage countered by uchimata
Kenka-yotsu

> **Keynote** Another study in avoidance, with all its attendant dangers and bonuses. Alexandra Schreiber of West Germany won the world middleweight title in Essen in 1987 by throwing the three-times world champion Brigitte Deydier (France) for *ippon* with exactly this technique.

b) I control and step over, maintaining my grips.

(d) Being in a kneeling position is no defence.

:) Now I am in a position to counter-attack.

(e) *Ippon!*

Morote-gari countered by uchimata

> **Keynote** This is a natural defence – it is just a twist and turn. And it works.

(c) I twist and turn, making the most of uke's own impetus.

(a) Uke ducks for *morote-gari*.

(d) In this case I have grabbed the arm and achieve quite good head control.

(b) I grab what I can – not a particularly scientific explanation, but true.

(e) I may only get *yuko*, but it puts me in good position on the ground.

Training

Uchimata is quite a complex action. Like many of judo's forward throws, the entry involves a fast, spinning motion that has to be executed with precision – ending with perfect balance on one leg. When you consider that this is all done in a moving, ever-changing situation against an opponent who is trying to stop you with every fibre of his being, it is amazing that uchimata works at all! That, of course, is part of the mystery and the success of judo. When viewed in this way, it is not surprising that many uchimata attacks do not succeed, or succeed only partially. But all uchimata specialists will vouch for the importance not only of regular practice, but intelligent use of that practice.

Attention paid to the basics is never wasted. This is as true in developing uchimata as in developing anything else. The dominating characteristic of Japanese education is to work on small details, progressing step by step (rather than settling down to work with the whole technique at once). There is much to be said for this approach. I spent hours working on my *hikite* pull for my *uchimata*, and I never regretted it – especially when finding myself in the final of the world championships!

So, it is quite a good idea to separate the component parts of *uchimata* like the *hikite* or *tsurite* pull, or the stepping motions, and to spend some time concentrating on each one before trying to piece them together as a whole. This is important in the early stages, when acquiring the skills of *uchimata*: ingraining the correct action, though it may appear somewhat laborious, will pay great dividends later on.

But it is equally important to maintain these very precise skills later on. Most people – of all ages – find that without regular *uchikomi* their technique deteriorates. While randori is an important tool in the shaping and developing of *uchimata*, too much randori alone can allow bad habits to creep in. So if you suddenly find that your *uchimata* has stopped working, or that your balance is not as good as it was, or that you can't even achieve the entry, take a training partner and spend a few hours going back over the basics. You will almost certainly be surprised by the bad habits that have crept into your actions without your noticing.

Here are some of the basic movements to work on.

Kuzushi

(a)

> **Keynote** I cannot emphasise enough the importance of *kuzushi*, or the breaking of balance. This is the best way to develop it.

(a) Standing with a partner, I step into the technique.

(b) From my base on my left foot, I pull high with my *hikite* (sleeve grip). At the same time, I effect a lift/pull with my *tsurite* hand. The word *tsurite* is traditionally related to the action of fishing, for it mimics that fishing-rod action. Both the *hikite* and *tsurite* pulls bring uke off his heels onto his toes, and create the possibility of the throw.

(b)

(c) Once I bring my right foot into position, uke is brought even more noticeably into the air. Having reached this point, I come out and start again. I do not want to complicate my practice with a full attacking action yet.

Note When I was in full training, I would do about twenty or thirty of these at the start of my practice, before randori. This kept the all-important *kuzushi* 'in tune' with the rest of the movement.

(c)

The steps

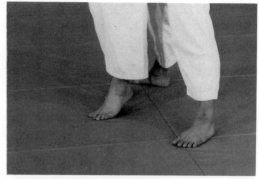

(c) I pivot on my left toes and having achieved the required hip/body contact, prepare to bring the lifting leg into play.

a) It is based on the traditional triangle. My left foot forms the peak of the triangle.

(d) I start to lift. Note that my standing leg is slightly bent: this is essential, because the best *uchimata* result comes when a slight spring is added to the process.

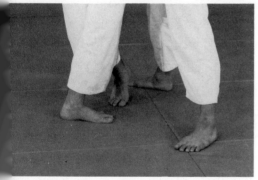

b) My right foot makes the semi-circle action. I tuck it in behind the left.

Now I am ready for my basic *uchikomi* movement. At Tokai University, I would do about three hundred *uchikomi* a day, in sets of thirty, before every practice. After a hard randori, I would do another hundred, just to iron out any bad habits. I would start slowly, but steadily, and gradually build up speed. Sometimes, I would end the session with special speed work. This involves thirty second periods, in which I would expect to do forty-seven or forty-eight full entries. I would do ten sets, with a minute's rest in between. It was a gruelling practice.

The spring

> **Keynote** The Japanese word for 'spring' is *haneru* – which is where we get the term *hane-goshi*. All kinds of *uchimata* require a springing action, though some (especially those using a lot of hip action) require more than others. This element too can only be instilled through systematic training.

(a)

(a) I want to introduce some movement into the *uchikomi* practice, so I pull forward and down in an attempt to establish a rhythm.
(b) I lift strongly - looking for a good *kuzushi*.
(c) I turn in using a spinning entry, and bounce uke into the air.
(d) Then I put him back down again.

Note I will do about thirty of these before each practice. It is quite demanding, but it is worth hundreds of just ordinary *uchikomi*. It calls for ninety per cent commitment.

(c)

Three-person uchikomi

> **Keynote** This is about developing strength and power in the whole *uchikomi* action. The third person pulls down on my uke, giving extra resistance, and thus forcing me to take my *kuzushi* and spring action to the limits of my capacity. I used to do a hundred of these every other day.

(a)

(b)

(c)

(d)

(a-d). Three person *uchikomi* – the Japanese expression is *sannin uchikomi*.

(b)

(d)

Solo uchikomi

Keynote

There are many things that can be done on your own. It is very helpful to work with a rubber inner tube tied round a pole to develop both the feeling of *kuzushi* and of turning in using the pull. I would do this twice or three times a week when I was competing, aiming for five or six sets of fifty repetitions.

It is also possible to use the space of a dojo to practise stepping actions, imagining you have hold of an uke. Through this, you can develop a freedom in your own movement, with a good degree of control over direction and purpose. You can make single attacks, or attacks in different directions; pull your imaginary opponent to one side or another, back or forward; you can attack with different combinations; or make adjustments for taller or smaller opponents. There are no limits – except those set by your imagination! To do this well, and with real purpose, is quite an advanced practice.

There are two types of wall solo uchikomi, which help concentrate the turning & lifting action one of which is illustrated here (a-c).

(a)

(b)

(c)

Weights

This is more of a personal footnote than practical advice. Most of my opponents during my competitive days said that they found me very strong. I didn't tell them, but at no point during my competitive career was I able to bench-press more than one hundred kilos. That is not very impressive for a 95 kilo man, but, frankly, I was never very interested in weight training. I always preferred doing *uchikomi*...

Competition Uchimata

Very few major championships take place without *uchimata* playing some memorable role in one way or another. Sometimes, it is an especially fine technique which just lives in the memory. At other times, the *uchimata* is the making of a new, or the downfall of an existing champion.

In fact it is one of the three great scoring throws of modern judo. If *seoi-nage*, and its many variations, is the top-scoring throw in Japan, *uchimata* is probably the most successful throw in the West. The reasons for this are not hard to find. For a start, the classic position for uke – in a defensive posture, slightly leaning forward with legs spread – is very commonly adopted voluntarily, and relatively easy to induce. Secondly, it can be said generally that the flexibility in the hips, which is such a hallmark of Japanese judo, is much more limited in Western fighters, making them much more susceptible to the inner-thigh attack.

Just as important, however, is the very nature of the throw. It is big, spectacular, and on the whole more difficult to counter than other throws off one leg. It is incumbent upon most champions to be able to produce at least one "big gun" in their throwing armoury, and the variety of entries for *uchimata* puts it high on the list of many fighters.

I wasn't the only person it served well in the 1987 world championships in Essen. Jae-Yup Kim, the 60k Korean had also used it in round after round as he progressed to the final to meet my compatriot, Shinji Hosokawa, who had won their final easily at the Los Angeles Olympics. Essen was to be a very different matter. For almost an hour before the final, Kim could be seen in the warm-up room, doing *uchikomi* – exclusively on *uchimata*. He started with three track-suit tops, discarding them one by one as he built up steam. Shortly before he was called to the final, he pulled off his last track suit and threw his partner a few more times with *uchimata*. Just seconds after the final started, he threw Hosokawa with *uchimata makikomi* for ippon. Clearly, the action, and the mental image, had been drilled so deeply into him that he was going to do *uchimata* whatever or whoever grabbed hold of him.

Essen showed *uchimata*'s effectiveness, whether it was in the lightweights or the heavyweights. In fact, a third final was also decided by *uchimata* when Alexandra Schreiber scooped the reigning world middleweight champion Brigitte Deydier (France) into the air with a strong leg action for ippon.

This *uchimata* season was to have an intriguing echo the following year in the Seoul Olympics. On two occasions, Hosokawa won spectacularly with *uchimata sukashi* – and many people concluded that he had been working on the technique because of the *uchimata* defeat the year before. (As it happened, Hosokawa lost at the semi-final stage and thefore didn't meet Kim in the final). Similarly, Theo Meijer, my Dutch opponent in the Essen final, won his first round with *uchimata sukashi*, and it crossed my mind that he had made a special study of the counter just in case we were to have a repeat encounter...though in the event we both lost before we could meet again.

It is not difficult to find champions who have relied on *uchimata* at every weight category. If Jae-Yup Kim was an example at u60k, Marc Alexandre (France) was an example at u65k, and later at u71k, when he won the Olympic title in Seoul. His *uchimata*, executed with a *tsugi-ashi* entry at very high speed proved effective at the 1984 Olympics and at many European championships. The 1989 world championships in Belgrade saw one of the quickest *uchimata* victories at the highest level, when Chang Soo Lee (North Korea) won his bronze medal by throwing Hungary's former European champion, Bertalan Hajtos for ippon with left *uchimata* in just 13 seconds, which was no mean feat.

It has been the leading technique for most of the u71k Russian fighters over the years, from Gennady Tenadze to Vladimir Dgebouadze, the world junior champion in 1990 at u71k, who won a bronze medal with *uchimata* in his first senior world championships in Barcelona in 1991. Another Russian to specialise in *uchimata* has been Bashir Varaev who has won four European titles in succession, though never quite managing to win an Olympic or world title. He exhibited the typical Russian style – reaching over for the belt when he could, or at least taking the back of the jacket, and powering his way in, lifting strongly with his leg, rather than with his hip.

The u78k category has produced a long line of fine *uchimata* stylists too, among them Britain's Neil Adams, who won the world title in 1981. In his first competition in Japan, when he was still competing at u71k, and largely unknown, he stunned a packed house at the Budokan by throwing Nishida, then one of the bright stars of Japanese judo, for ippon with *uchimata*. It was one of those rare moments in a judo career when inspiration seemed to appear from nowhere. Adams remembers: "I attacked Nishida with *tai-otoshi* a couple of times, but he just stepped over. Suddenly, for no real reason, I switched to *uchimata*. Nishida thought another *tai-otoshi* was coming and just stepped over it – only to be caught in mid-air and planted squarely on his back. It was a combination I never forgot, and one I used many times over the next decade."

Another stylish u78k fighter, Bernard Tchoullyan (France) has cause to remember *uchimata* after being on the end of one in a notable 28 second fight in the Moscow Olympics. He met Juan Ferrer (Cuba) in the semi-finals, and threw him easily with *ippon-seoi-nage* for *waza-ari* in 12 seconds. He looked as if he was going to cruise through to the final, but 16 seconds later was himself thrown – for *ippon* with *uchimata*. It is the kind of throw that can produce very unexpected reversals.

Peter Seisenbacher, Austria's double Olympic champion also used *uchimata* – though as a second string to his main throw, *osoto-gari*. His preferred method was to pull his opponent's head down, and as uke forced his head up, suddenly whip in for *uchimata*.

One of my predecessors at light-heavyweight was Tomio Sasahara. He won the world title twice, in 1969 in Mexico City, and then again in 1971 in Ludwigshafen, West Germany (when the weight limit for the category was 93k). In the 1971 event, he won all his contests with ippon – using *uchimata*.

Both Yasuhiro Yamashita and Hitoshi Saito of Japan used *uchimata* frequently during their contest careers, which brought them Olympic and world titles, and the All-Japan Championships, though their styles were very different. Yamashita (along with Seisenbacher and myself) belonged to the group who would prefer to pull their opponents on to the throw, while Saito (along with Adams and Alexandre) preferred to push his opponents to achieve his entry. It is an important distinction.

Uchimata was not so often seem in women's judo in the early years of top international competition. This was partly because the throw calls for a strong, explosive action which took time to develop; and partly because women's judo, by its very nature, was less rigid or stiff than men's. As women's judo grew however, training patterns, including the use of weights, meant the introduction of more throws such as *uchimata*, *osoto-gari* and *harai-goshi* – throws from one standing leg calling for powerful use of arms and a lifting action. There were some notable exceptions even in that first decade, the most famous being Belgium's light-heavyweight Ingrid Berghmans. She had a very elegant *uchimata* which involved pulling her opponent round on to her hip in a manner not unlike nage-no-kata style. She achieved some superb results with this year after year.

Her example meant that by 1988, when women's judo appeared on the Olympic calendar for the first time, albeit as a demonstration sport, *uchimata* had become a high-scoring *shiai* technique. Berghmans herself used it as she won the u72k category title; and so did Britain's world champion Diane Bell (u61k), who although known as a *seoi-nage* specialist produced a superb left *uchimata* on Noriko Mochida to win her category.

Since it first took its place in the main catalogue of judo throws, *uchimata* has always been one of the most powerful of them. And although judo is always changing, there is little doubt that *uchimata* will retain its importance as a dynamic international match winner.

Above: Marc Alexandre of France scores ippon with uchimata on his way to the under 71k Olympic title in Seoul 1988.

Frank Wieneke of West Germany scores a fine ippon with a circling uchimata against the unorthodox Gonzalez of Spain, despite his opponent's stiff defensive left arm.

ne of the great uchimata stylists, Jae-Yup Kim of Korea scores a palpable ippon on Madhar f Surinam on his way to the u60k Olympic gold in Seoul, 1988.

Masahiko Okuma of Japan scoring ippon on Daniel May of Holland with uchimata in the 1991 world championships in Barcelona. Note the high collar grip, allowing the Japanese fighter to control his opponent's head. The Dutch fighter had a cross grip immediately prior to being thrown and had his stance reversed, (although holding with a left cross grip, he was standing with his right leg forward). This is normally a defensive posture, but in this instance, not an effective one.

Above: superb hip and leg action from a French fighter, Tournoi de Paris 1989.

Even experts get countered sometimes: Bashir Varaev of the Soviet Union, four times European champion, miscalculated against Daniel Lascau of Germany in the 1991 world championships in Barcelona and was hoisted high into the air with an impressive uranage. Despite twisting out of the throw, ippon was given.

Uchimata makikomi is increasingly popular in women's judo. Noriko Mochida of Japan throws Donna Guy of New Zealand, Olympic Games, Seoul, 1988.

Total committment by Fabienne Boffin of France as she throws Gavrilova of the Soviet Union, Prague, European championships, 1991.

Yamamoto of Japan attacks Lorenzo of Spain with uchimata in the 1989 Tournoi de Paris, but the Spaniard's supple defence frustrates him, forcing him to makikomi.

Barbara Eickoff of Austria scores ippon with a dynamic uchimata. European championships, Pamplona, 1988.

Only desperate, cat-like twisting prevented this attack from scoring higher than a yuko. The thrower, Val of Belgium, has attacked well, but his opponent has just managed to free his left arm and head, allowing him to avoid conceding ippon.

Above: Bozo of France scores ippon with a typically European power- style uchimata, forcing his opponent's head down as he jacks up the leg. Below: his awareness of uchimata extends to a practised defence against the same being done to him. Both pictures Tournoi de Paris 1989.

France's Bruno Carabetta, was caught in the opening seconds of his third contest in the 1988 Seoul Olympic Games in the under 65k category, by Nigeria's Omagbaluwaji. The referee awarded ippon, but was overruled by the judges who declared it a waza-ari. Carabetta eventually won, and went on to reach the final, but this uchimata almost caused a major upset.

*Torsten Brechot of East Germany throwing Baylon of the Phillipines for ippon with uchimata.
Note the high double lapel grip controlling the shorter man's head, and the way Brechot hooks
his opponent's knee with his heel. Seoul Olympic Games, 1988.*

*Brechot again. This time his opponent is the defending champion, Frank Wieneke of West
Germany. Wieneke is airborne, but he succeeds in breaking the hikite grip, a vital part of most
effective defences against uchimata.*

Sven Loll of East Germany, on his way to an Olympic silver medal in Seoul 1988, using his long arms and legs to good effect, attacks with ken-ken (hopping) uchimata. Note the elbow lifting up and the extension of the legs.

Diane Bell, though better known for her right seoi-nage, totally surprised her Japanese opponent, Noriko Mochida, by producing this left uchimata in the Olympic final. Although Mochida tried to land on her front, Bell pulled her round strongly with the sleeve grip, putting the Japanese player flat on her back for ippon. Seoul, 1988.

Uchimata by Marc Alexandre of France. His opponent only avoids a major score by letting go with both hands and spinning into a sort of desperate handstand.

Vladimir Dgebouadze of the Soviet Union demolishes Masimo Sulli of Italy. (see opposite)

*In the Barcelona world championships Dgebouadze scored two ippons on Sulli of Italy with a
very unusual circling ken-ken uchimata. The referee called matte during the course of the first
attack and the throw was disallowed. Ten seconds later he just did it again, and this time ippon
was awarded. Note how he uses the mid-back grip to drive Sulli's head to the tatami as he hops.*

Grigory Veritchev of the Soviet Union, 1987 world heavyweight champion, throws Kusmuk of Yugoslavia for waza-ari in the Seoul Oympic Games with a fine hip-throw uchimata.

The great danger with any over-zealous uchimata attack is that of neck injury, a fact which led to the head dive style of uchimata being banned. Effectively the thrower would pin his opponent's body to him and attempt to somersault with his opponent on his back. Usually he would end up doing a sort of headstand which was i. some cases fatal. Here William Cusack of Scotland risks injury and disqualification as he attempts to topple h his opponent to defeat.

Quellmalz of East Germany scores decisively with an arm over the back grip.

Double Olympic gold medallist Hitoshi Saito of Japan attacks Henry Stohr of East Germany.

Neil Adams of Great Britain using a high collar grip to throw Hennevald of Holland for ippon.

Yasuhiro Yamashita, world and Olympic champion, and Japan's most successful fighter in the 1970s and 1980s, throws Robert van de Walle (Belgium) for ippon in the Open category of the 1981 world championships in Maastricht.

Index

Other titles now available from Ippon Books in the Judo Masterclass Techniques series:

Armlocks   by   Neil Adams
Ashiwaza   by   Nobuyuki Sato
Grips   by   Neil Adams
Harai-goshi   by   Jean-Luc Rouge
Osoto-gari   by   Yasuhiro Yamashita
Tomoe-nage   by   Katsuhiko Kashiwazaki